THE BIBLICAL ALPHABET

Words by Robin Feiner

A is for **A**braham.
Born after the great flood,
this nomadic leader of the
Jewish people was the first
person to teach us that there
was only one God. Before
Abraham, people believed
in many gods and even
worshipped idols.

B is for John the **B**aptist. God brought John into the world for a special purpose. He was to prepare people for the Messiah's coming. <u>After he baptized Jesus, John watched the Holy Spirit descend upon Him</u>.

C is for Jesus **C**hrist.
From a miracle birth to a miracle resurrection, Jesus of Nazareth lived his life as a religious teacher and died for humankind's sins on a cross. He was the Son of God, the cornerstone of Christianity and the greatest biblical hero of all.

D is for **D**avid.
This small, unassuming shepherd became God's chosen king due to his bravery and unwavering faith. He brought down the bully, Goliath, with one well-placed stone between the giant's eyes, and proved that might doesn't always equal right.

E is for Eve.
Created out of Adam's rib
to be his companion, Eve
lived with Adam in the
perfection of the Garden
of Eden ... until she was
tempted by Satan to eat the
forbidden fruit, which she
also gave to Adam. This was
humankind's original sin.

F is for **F**elix the Procrastinator. When confronted by the Apostle Paul preaching God's word, this Roman Governor of Judea reportedly began to "tremble in fear." Felix was so rattled by Paul's righteousness that he had to send Paul away to be dealt with later.

G is for the **G**ospels.
Told through the eyes of four
different men – Matthew, Mark,
Luke and John – the Gospels
document the life of Jesus.
Sharing the Good News, and
preaching the Christian
principles of love and kindness.

H is for **H**agar.
This handmaid had a difficult time when she became pregnant with Abraham's child. She ran away but was stopped by an angel, who told her that her unborn son, Ishmael, had a very important destiny. He would later become a key figure in Islam.

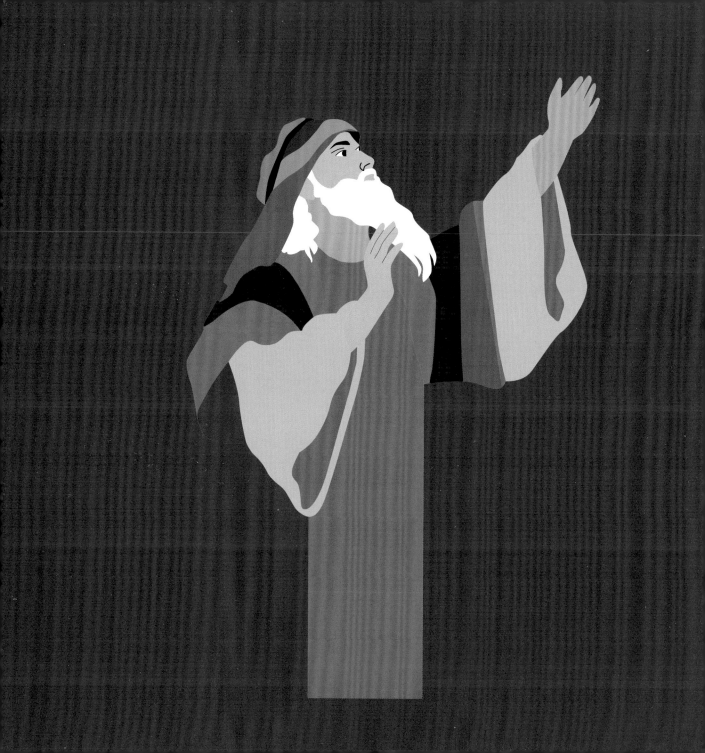

I is for Isaiah.
Widely regarded as one
of the greatest prophets in
the Bible, Isaiah saw a vision
of God and offered to be
His messenger. "Here am I.
Send me!" He prophesized
the coming of the Messiah
700 years before Jesus
was born.

J is for **Joseph**.
Favored by his father, Joseph was given a colorful coat to wear. This enraged his 11 brothers, who sold him in Egypt as a slave. Joseph later won favor with Pharaoh for his ability to interpret dreams, and went on to rule Egypt.

K is for **K**ing Solomon. Known for being the wisest man who ever lived – and also the most foolish – Solomon was the son of King David. He ruled Israel with great wisdom before losing his way and succumbing to the temptations of money and power.

L is for Daniel in the Lions' den. Condemned to the lions' den for praying to his own God, Daniel's powerful prayers were answered when God sent an angel to close the lions' jaws to protect him. This proved to the non-believers that Daniel's God was great.

M is for **M**oses.
One of the Old Testament's greatest prophets, Moses led the Israelites out of slavery and to the Promised Land. After wearing Pharaoh down with the 10 plagues, Moses miraculously parted the Red Sea. He later received God's 10 Commandments atop Mount Sinai.

N is for **N**oah.
When God resolved to wipe
a sinful mankind from the face
of the earth by bringing a flood,
he chose Noah as his designated
survivor. Noah built an ark and
filled it with one pair of every
animal species, and lived to
tell the tale.

O is for Onesimus.
A slave to Philemon, Onesimus ran away and was imprisoned in Rome. There he met Paul the Apostle, who baptized him, took him under his wing and asked Philemon to forgive his escape. Onesimus's Christian journey saw him go from slave to saint.

Pp

P is for Peter and Paul.
These two influential defenders
of the faith are often referred
to as the Chief Apostles because
they spread the gospel of
Christ far and wide. At a time
when it was dangerous to be
a Christian, they stayed true
to the Word of Jesus and
converted many.

Q is for the **Q**ueen of Sheba. This strong female leader traveled from the far reaches of the world to witness the renowned wisdom of King Solomon. With her, she brought many valuable gifts and enjoyed lively conversations with the king to test his brilliance.

R is for Ruth.
After Naomi lost her husband
and two of her sons, her
widowed daughter-in-law,
Ruth, stayed by her side and
went with her to Bethlehem.
"Your people will be my
people," Ruth declared loyally.
She went on to become
David's great-grandmother.

S is for Samson.
This Hebrew warrior's source of strength was his long, uncut hair. His infamous demise came when he fell in love with Delilah, and revealed to her the secret of his strength. He awoke one day to find that Delilah had cut his hair while he slept, rendering him powerless.

T is for the Three Wise Men. When news spread that the son of God had been born in a manger, these three kings from the Orient followed the star to Bethlehem to pay their respects. They famously brought gifts of gold, frankincense and myrrh for baby Jesus.

U is for Job of **U**z.
Job was a good man who was gravely tested. Even after losing all his children, his cattle and his health, Job clung to his faith, and so God rewarded him richly in the land of Uz.

Vv

V is for the **V**irgin Mary.
The angel Gabriel appeared
to this young virgin and told
her she would bear a son
conceived "in the Holy Spirit."
Mary had faith enough to
receive God's blessing and
nine months later the savior,
Jesus Christ, was born in
Bethlehem.

W is for Jonah and the **W**hale. When Jonah refused God's call and fled, God sent a storm to tip him out of his boat and he was swallowed by a whale. While in the belly of the whale for three days, Jonah prayed for God's forgiveness and was coughed up, alive and unharmed.

X is for Xerxes and Queen Esther. Xerxes was a Persian king and Esther was his wife. When the king's chief advisor, Haman, plotted to have all the Jews in the kingdom killed, Esther foiled his plan because she was secretly Jewish! This is the basis for Purim, a celebration in the Jewish faith.

Y is for **Y**ahweh.
When God instructed Moses
to lead the Israelites out
of Egypt, Moses asked,
"Who shall I say told me?"
God replied that it is I,
"Yahweh." Yahweh is a spirit
that is infinite, eternal, and
unchangeable in its being,
wisdom, power, holiness,
justice, goodness and truth.

Z is for **Z**acchaeus.
This wealthy tax collector climbed a tree to get a better view of Jesus, who then singled him out for a home visit. Inspired by Jesus and his teachings, Zacchaeus pledged to give half his wealth to the poor and be a better person from then on.

The ever-expanding legendary library

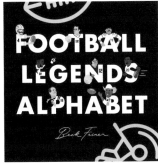

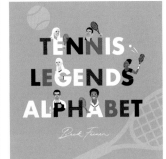

EXPLORE THESE LEGENDARY ALPHABETS & MORE AT WWW.ALPHABETLEGENDS.COM

THE BIBLICAL ALPHABET (2ND EDITION)
www.alphabetlegends.com

Published by Alphabet Legends Pty Ltd in 2020
Created by Beck Feiner
Copyright © Alphabet Legends Pty Ltd 2020

UNICEF AUSTRALIA
A portion of the Net Proceeds from the sale of this book
are donated to UNICEF.

9 780648 506324